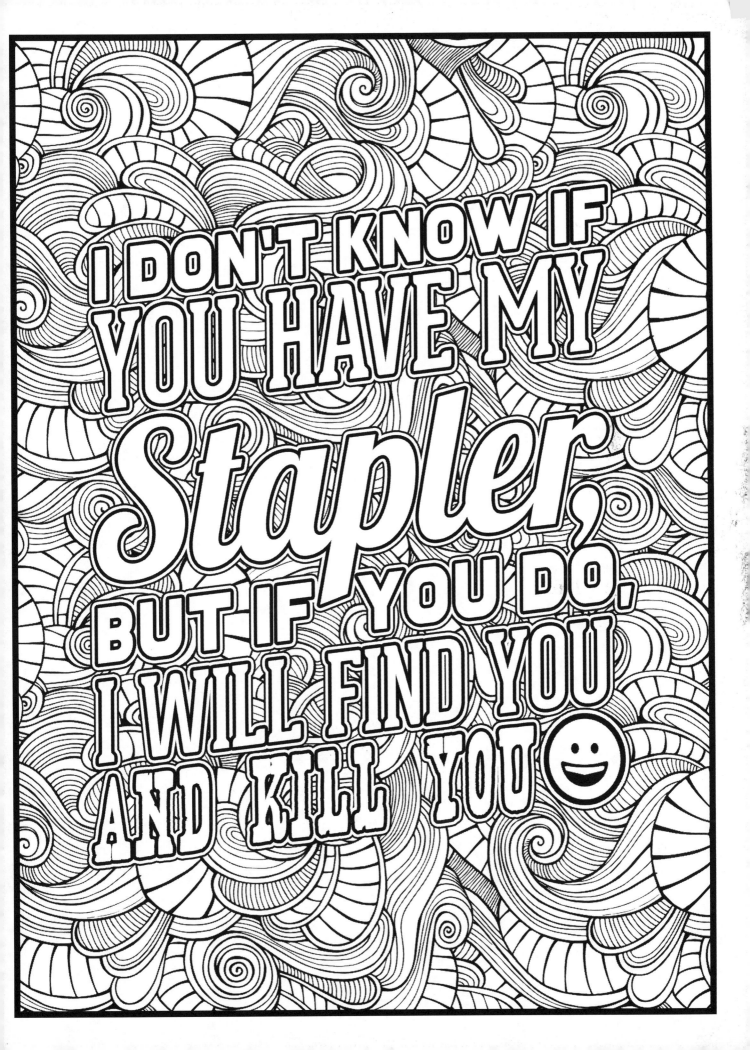

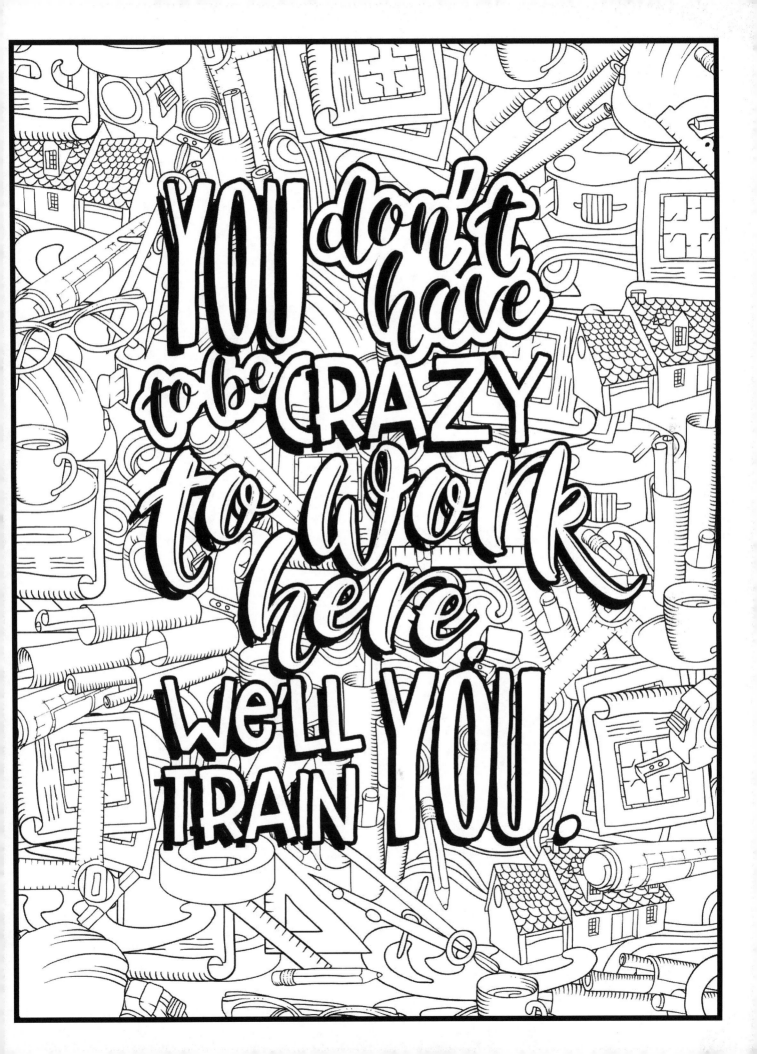

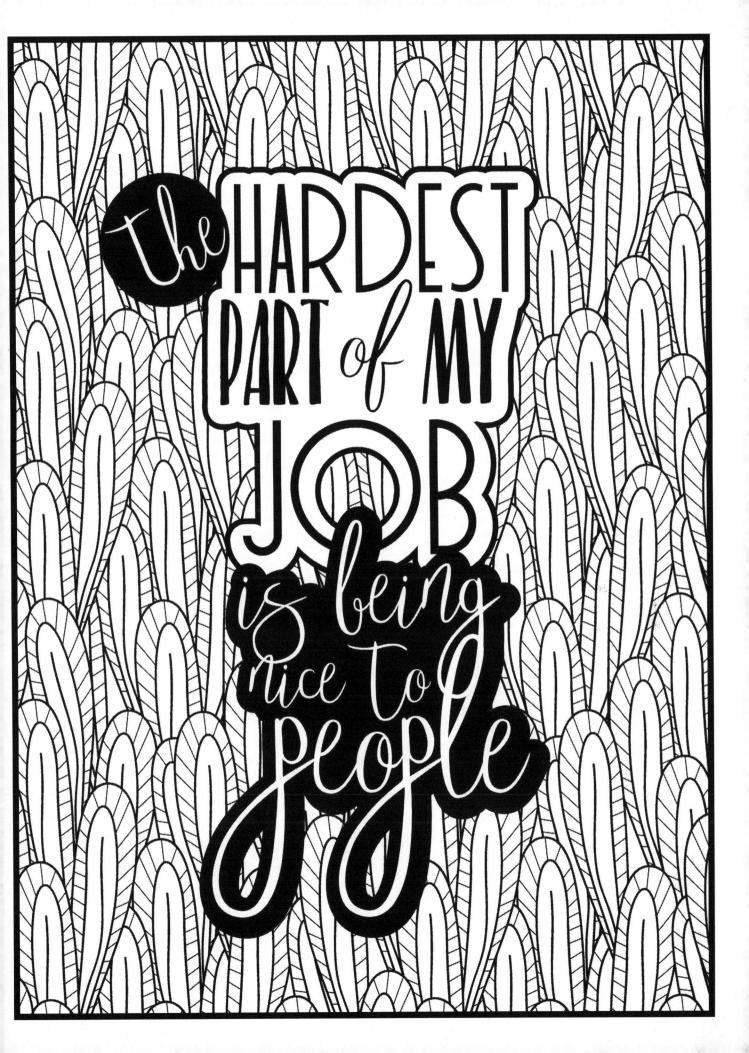

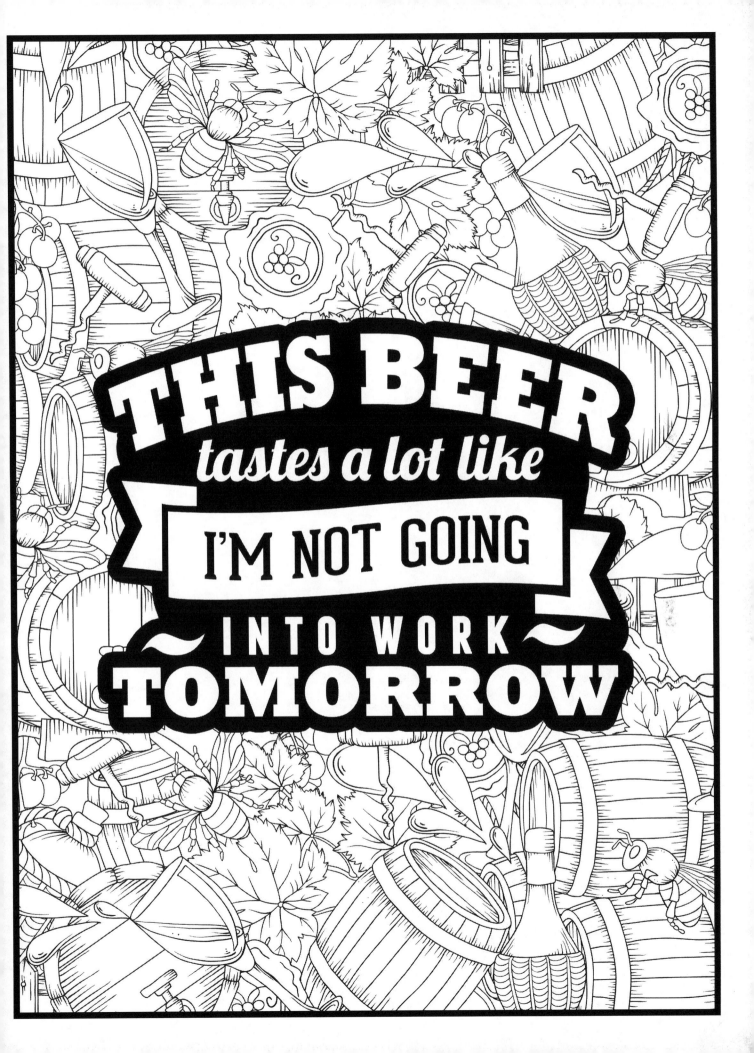

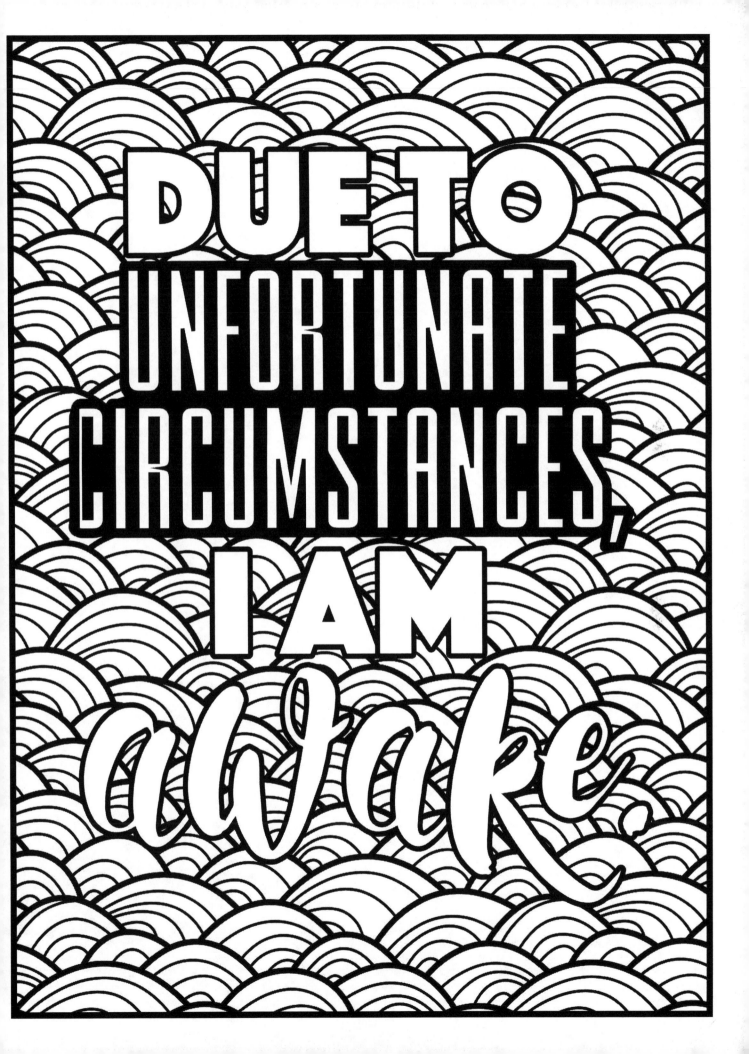

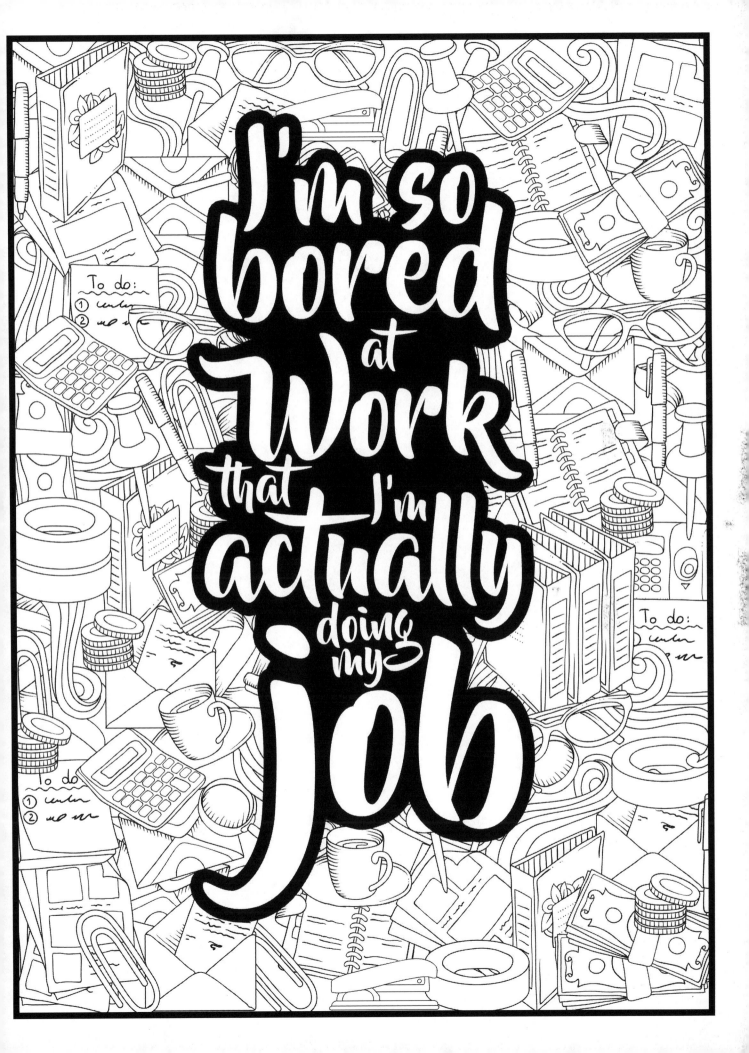

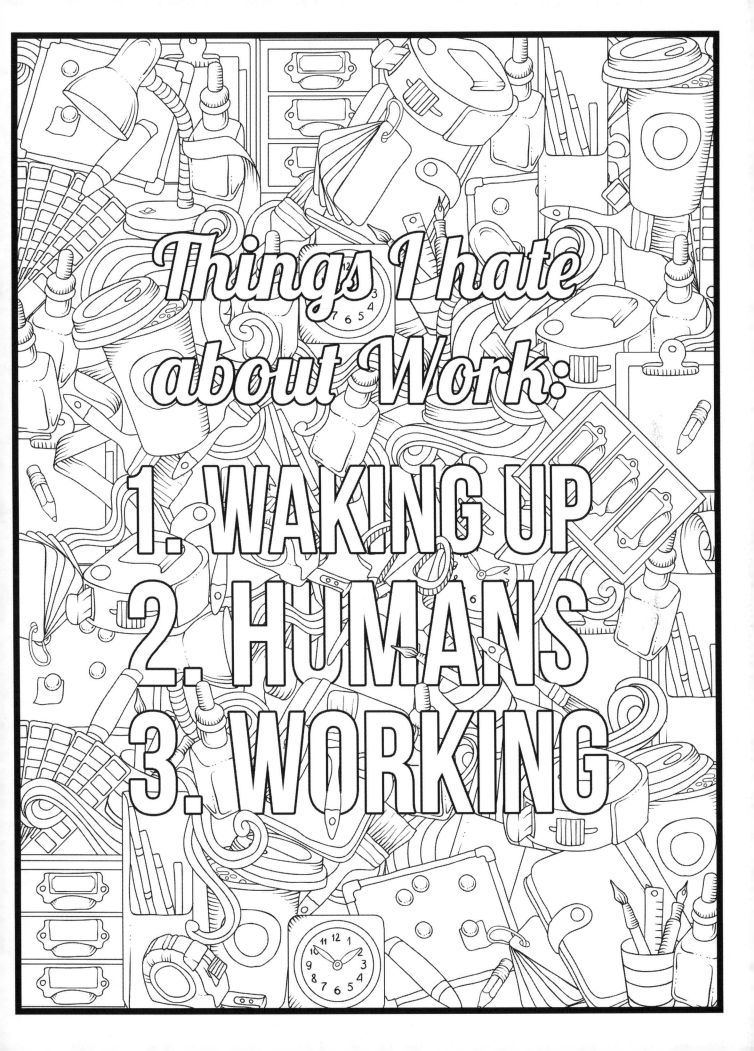

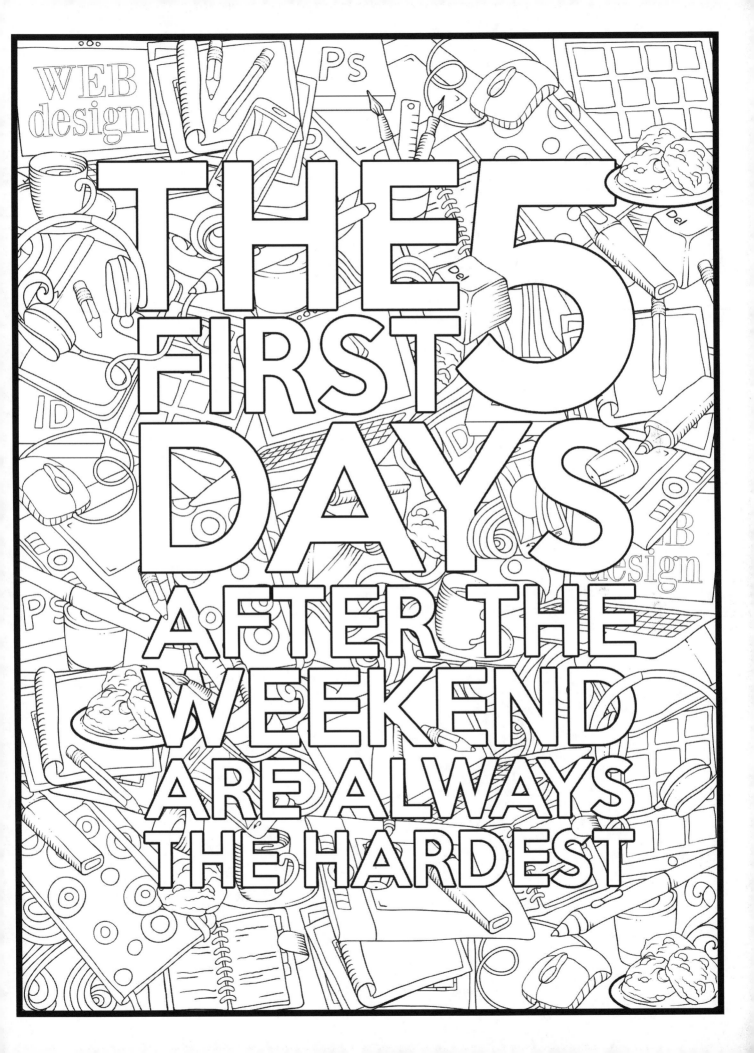

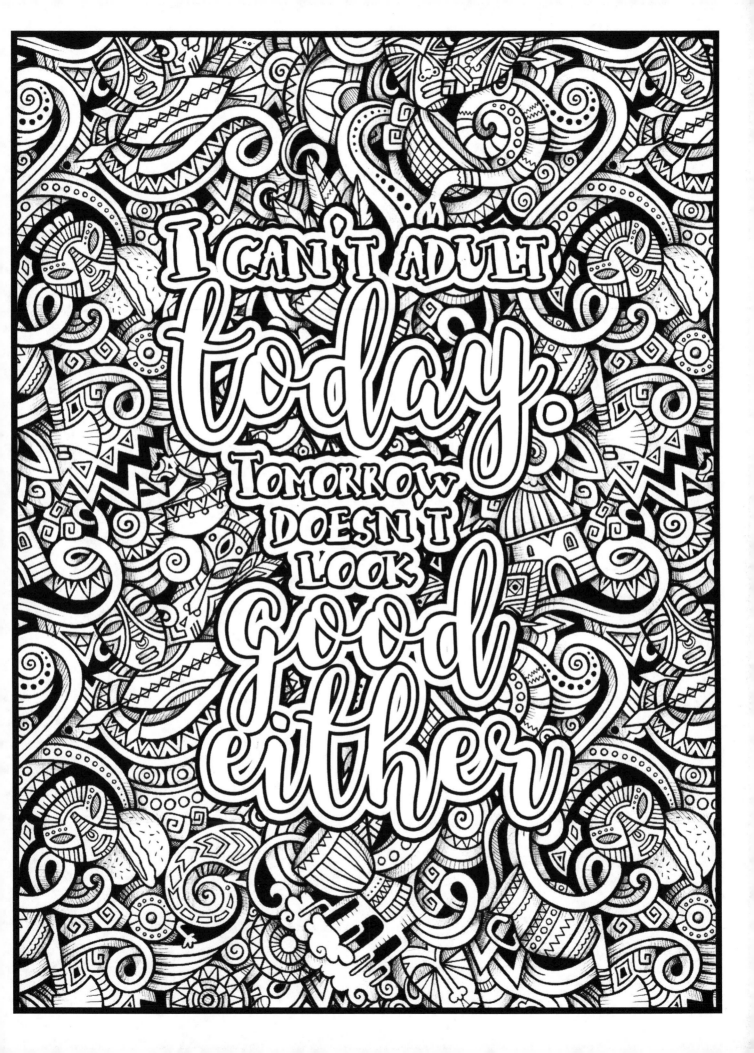

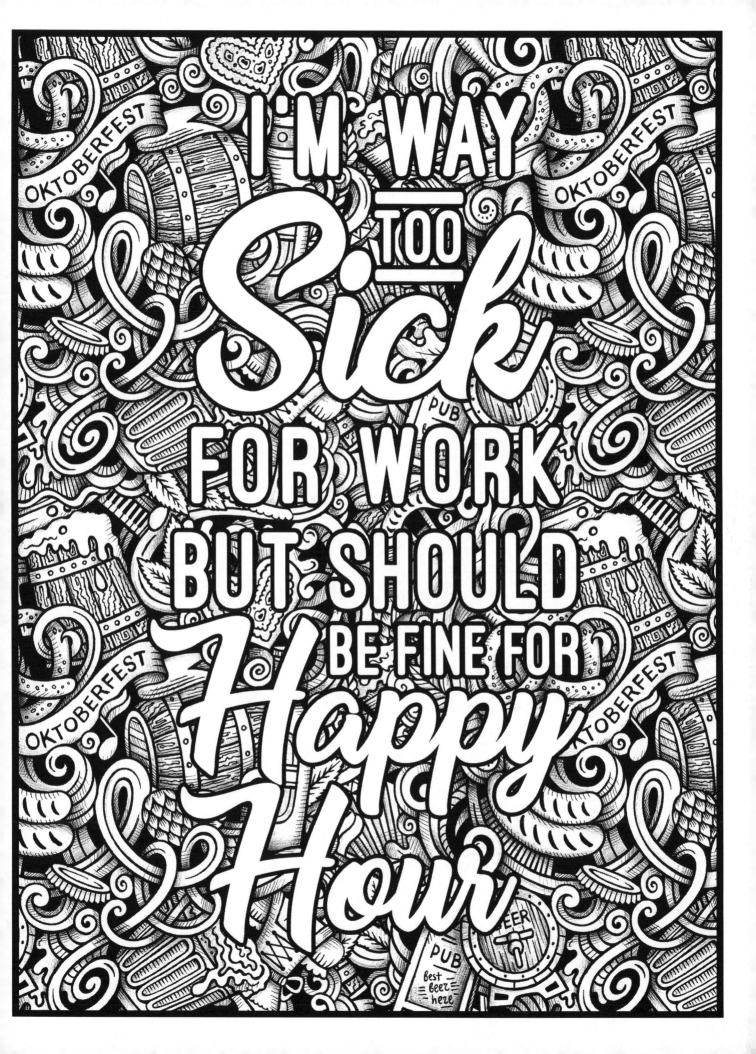

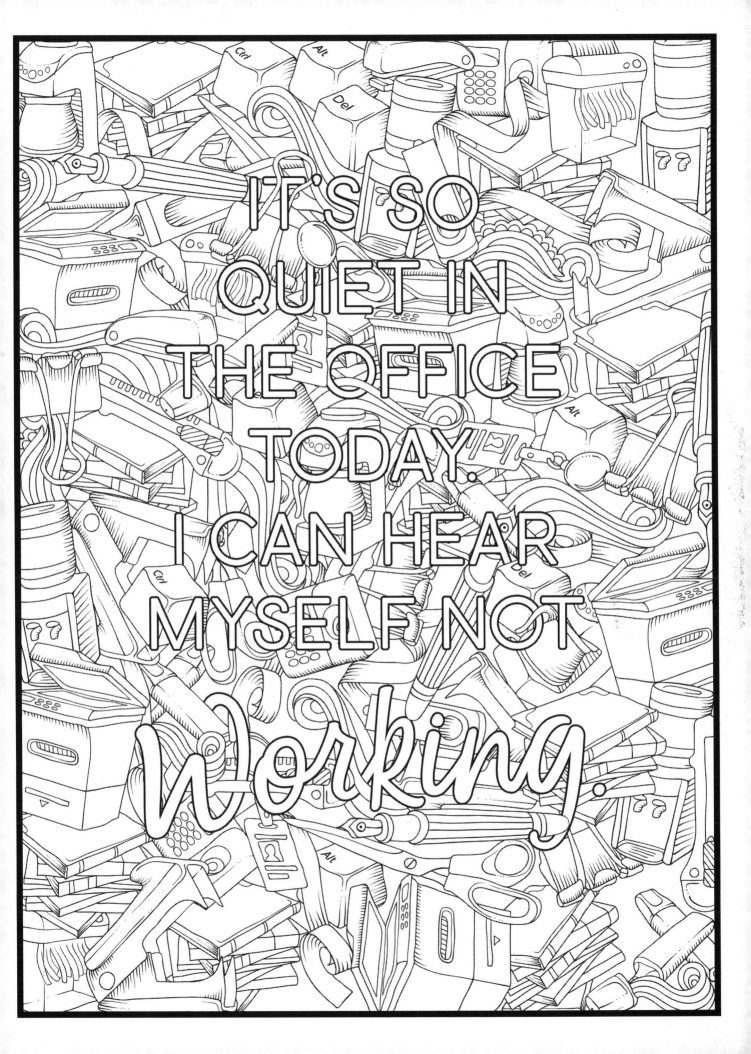

THANK YOU *student loans* FOR HELPING ME
GET THROUGH COLLEGE
I DON'T THINK I CAN EVER
Repay You

BE SURE TO FOLLOW US
ON SOCIAL MEDIA FOR THE
LATEST NEWS, SNEAK
PEEKS, & GIVEAWAYS

[Instagram] @PapeterieBleu

[Facebook] Papeterie Bleu

[Twitter] @PapeterieBleu

ADD YOURSELF TO OUR MONTHLY
NEWSLETTER FOR FREE DIGITAL
DOWNLOADS AND DISCOUNT CODES

www.papeteriebleu.com/newsletter

CHECK OUT OUR OTHER BOOKS!

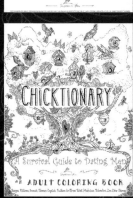